<u>Love Magic for Beginners</u>

<u>Reflections, Meditations, Rituals and Methods</u>

Contact: www.HarryEilenstein.de
Harry.Eilenstein@web.de
Harry Eilenstein at youtube

Production and publishing house: BoD – Books on Demand, Norderstedt

ISBN: 9783753461816

Table of Contents

I Love Spells

Love spells, along with hunting spells, fertility spells, damage spells, omens, oracles and otherworld journeys, are among the forms of magic that can be found in almost all ancient cultures – relationships have always been a central theme and closeness, love, sex and companionship have also been basic needs in people's lives in earlier times.

Although there are several variations of the love spell, the basic forms are still largely the same in all cultures:

- the love amulet,
- the request to the gods,
- the command to the spirits,
- the magical compulsion and
- the love potion or love food.

These five variants already show the range of the basic attitude of the one who performs such a love spell: It ranges from the manumitting request to the compulsion.

I 1. the love amulet

The amulet or the talisman is an object which is magically effective because of its symbolism or because of the signs painted on it. In most cases, the amulet is made by a specialist, that is, by a sorcerer or a witch.

Often it is also made of certain metals (copper for Venus, etc.) or at certain times (often at full moon).

I 2. The petition to the gods

The petition to the gods is generally a more manumitting method, even if the petitioner assumes that his request will be granted. It is performed either by the person himself or again by a specialist – usually within the framework of a ritual.

I 3. The command to the spirits

The command to the spirits can be given when the person has a means of pressure with which he can make the spirits do what he wants. This may simply be his will or his threat of a deity's wrath, withdrawal of offerings, or even destruction of the spirit's cult.

The nature of the spirits in this method can be very diverse, ranging from animal spirits to ancestors to demigods. This method will be used almost exclusively by "professionals".

I 4. The magical compulsion

The magical compulsion is a direct intervention in the situation – not an indirect request or demand to gods or spirits, nor an amulet that is supposed to fulfill the wishes of the person concerned in a mostly undefined way.

The main method used here are sigil magic, in which a wish is sent out with high concentration, and also hypnosis or remote hypnosis.

These methods can also be practiced only by an experienced magician or an experienced witch. In these methods, the desired woman or man is usually mainly an object, but does not appear more than an equal counterpart – as is the case with most "invitation love spells".

I 5. The love potion

The love potion is a specialty of Indo-European cultures, which originated from the reinterpretation of the ritual potion.

The very old idea that the arrival in the otherworld after death is just as much a birth as the arrival at the beginning of life in this world, has been differentiated already in the early Neolithic period to a re-procreation, a re-birth and a re-breastfeeding. Thereby the beyond goddess has become the re-conception mistress, the re-birth mother and the re-breastfeeding nurse.

The milk of the goddess at the re-breastfeeding has become in the cult of the early Indo-Europeans the ritual potion which will have represented at first the security with the goddess. In the course of time, however, this potion has been reinterpreted as the means giving rebirth, i.e. immortality in the next world. In this way, the nectar ambrosia of the Greeks and the soma amrita of the Indians (both literally mean "immortality potion"), as well as the haoma of the Persians and the ritual mead of the Celts and Germanic tribes have been created. From this eventually developed the search for the elixir of life of the alchemists in Europe and India.

From the combination of the re-procreation, in which the afterlife goddess is the re-procreation lover of the dead, and the ritual potion, which is connected with this re-procreation (and the rebirth following it), the "love potion" developed, which leads to the union of a man with a woman – originally these were the dead and the afterlife goddess.

II Analysis

One can have a violent desire and just dash off, using all the spells one knows. Then something will certainly happen – but not necessarily what one has longed for.

You can also pause first, if the suffering is very great, but cannot easily be dissolved, or if the desire is very violent, but cannot simply be fulfilled spontaneously – and then look a little more closely at what situation you are actually in.

So: first diagnosis, then therapy.

II 1. One's own character

Every person has his own character and therefore sees the world and the meaningful behavior in it differently than other people. It is therefore helpful to know oneself and also to know, at least roughly, how different people's views of the world can be.

If one knows that one seeks harmony above all, or that one is out for adventure, or that one simply wants to have one's way, one can direct one's own actions more clearly than if one did not have this self-knowledge at one's disposal. The clearer and more differentiated this self-knowledge is, the more effective one's own actions and consequently one's own magic will be.

From one's own character, including one's own values, it also depends, among other things, which methods one will use in magic: the friendly request to the gods or the command to the spirits, the striving for a general wish fulfillment or for a very concrete event, one's own magical action or the order to a magic professional, etc.

II 2. Analysis of the situation

When you want to achieve something and it is not immediately possible to do so effortlessly, it is usually helpful to take a closer look at what you want to achieve.

To do this, one can ask oneself a few questions, and the following selection could be expanded considerably without much effort:

"Do I already know this situation well? Have I experienced it many times before? What happened in these situations? How did they turn out? What did I actually want to happen?"

These questions can help to recognize possibly existing patterns in one's life, which one just possibly does not want to repeat for the seventeenth time.

If you find that you always experience the same things and that other people do not experience these things all the time as well, there is a very good chance that the occurrence of these repetitive events has its origin in you. In this case it is probably not very productive to experience the same thing a seventeenth time.

It would probably be much more effective to take a closer look at one's own pattern of experience – including its first occurrence and especially the feelings associated with this pattern. The healing and transformation of the feelings in this experience-pattern is in such a case what will bear much more pleasant fruits than the seventeenth repetition of the same experience – with a usually increasing intensity of the disaster at the end of these repetitions.

"Is my wish a relaxed 'Yes!'-wish or is it a tense 'Yes, but ...'-wish?"

In magic, never only the wish formulated and sent out is implemented, but always this wish together with all the important associations that one carries within oneself to this wish. Thus, one always receives a reflection of the entire image that one carries within oneself on the subject in question.

For magical practice this means that one should be careful to send out only one-pointed wishes, but no wishes to which one carries a contradiction within oneself – because this contradiction will also be a component of what life will send oneself as an answer to one's own wish.

If you find these contradictions in the magical wish fulfillment okay, you don't need to worry about them any further – but if you suffer from this "sting in the tail" that these wish fulfillments constantly have, you should take care to resolve all inner contradictions in order to get wish fulfillments that are not flawed.

With "contradiction" are here meant such inner constellations like "I want! – And I definitely don't want!". This can happen, for example, out of longing for closeness and simultaneous fear of closeness. Doing magic out of such an attitude is like standing with one foot on the gas pedal and with the other on the handbrake – this does no good to the engine.

There are also contradictions that are not contradictions – they occur mainly with square aspects in one's horoscope. In such a case you want two things at the same time, which are opposite and at least at first sight exclude each other.

For example, with a square between Pluto and Saturn, you want to be able to do what you want at any time (Pluto), but still have security in a relationship (Saturn). This kind of (apparent) contradiction requires above all sincerity, courage and creativity to find together with another person a way of life in which both have their place.

"Do I want a relationship, a love affair, or an erotic adventure in general – or do I want to live and experience these things with someone very specific?"

The answer to this question determines to a great extent the kind of love spell that is needed: With a general wish, you invite the experience in question and see what the "meaningful coincidence" then brings you – with the concrete wish, you put pressure on another person to do what you yourself want them to do.

While most people will find the invitation love spell acceptable, a great many people will find the compulsion love spell reprehensible. However, if you take a closer look at people's behavior, you will find that people have very different ideas of boundaries, of healthy self-assertion, of "encroaching responsibility", of "rightful claim on the other", and like things.

The boundary between "invitation" and "coercion" is by no means as clear and distinct and the same for everyone as one might at first think.

It makes sense to take a closer look at both of these types of love spells, as well as your own situation and your own standards for what you consider proper behavior and what you consider unacceptable.

For example, there are people for whom insistent persuasion and light physical pressure is perfectly normal, while others would already consider this an abuse. Moreover, in every culture there is a different kind of general definition of what is acceptable and what is unacceptable behavior – in everyday life and consequently also in the application of love spells.

"What exactly is my desire? To which of the astrological planets does this desire belong?"

To put it bluntly, not all love spells are the same – and one person's motivation for a love spell may be very different from another person's motivation for a love spell.

One can divide the common motivations into five categories, of which the first three are the most important:

- Moon: the desire for closeness, warmth and security
- Venus: being in love and in lovesickness
- Mars: the desire for sex

- Jupiter: to live a life together
- Saturn: needing a firm hold in life

The other five astrological planets could also be a possible motivation, but they occur rather rarely:

- Mercury:	to have conversations together with the other person
- Sun:	needing the other person for self-expression
- Uranus:	experiencing new things together
- Neptune:	to have mystical-symbiotic experiences together
- Pluto:	to feel that the other person is the center of one's own life

It immediately suggests itself to take a closer look at the respective desire, to consider its history in one's own life and to see what one actually wants by this disere – and whether what one wants is really the primary, original and actual desire.

This contemplation also already gives a first orientation, which planet one could ask for help with a possible love spell.

"Am I looking for the ideal relationship?"

Here the approach is very simple: If oneself is inwardly whole and free of contradictions and lives this radiantly outwardly, there will also be the people in one's life who exactly fit this own radiant center – living together with them will be a constant joy.

If you yourself are not in a healthy state, not free of contradictions, life with the help of the people you are dealing with will also reflect this state to you: If you live in an inner lack, you will meet people who also live in lack – and you will fight about everything out of the feeling of lack.

In this case, the solution is simple in approach and difficult in implementation: one will find the ideal relationship when one has healed oneself and lets what one really is shine uninhibitedly.

"Is it about conflicts in an already existing relationship or in a concrete aspired relationship?"

In this case, there are differences between the two people, one or possibly both of whom are seeking a relationship. Here the same applies as for the previous question: The other person reflects to you what is still wounded in yourself. Therefore, there is little point in trying to change the other person – in this case only self-healing can bring progress.

- - -

One does not necessarily have to share the view presented here on the situations in which love spells are usually performed – we are all much too different for that.

What counts in the end are one's own experiences. So there is something to be said for simply trying things out to see what effect they have. There is nothing that is a better foundation for one's own view of the world and for one's own action strategies than one's own experience …

This also applies to love spells.

II 3. Closeness

The design, the production, the dynamics and the effect of a love spell depend very much on what the person wants to achieve.

The theme of "closeness" usually shows up as "Without the other person, my life is meaningless!" and "I can't live without the other person!" This is very clearly a dependency and addiction symptom – which is one of the most common causes of suicide. And an addiction as a motivation for a love spell can actually only lead to disaster …

If the spell is unsuccessful, the person will only get more desperate – and if the spell is successful, the addiction will soon show itself as a massive disturbing factor in the new relationship.

So it would make more sense not to ask the moon for closeness in a relationship, but to ask the moon first of all for inner fullness. More precisely, you can also ask for the encounters and experiences that lead you to healing yourself.

It also makes a big difference whether one performs a moon love spell for more closeness in general and manumitting or whether one performs such a love spell with the wish for closeness to a very specific person. In the first case, the chances of a result that can be enjoyed are much greater.

Something else would be a moon love spell, which has only the task to meet again a person, whom you once knew and whom you would like to have in your life again (if the finding again by Internet etc. is not possible). Why not … but you will see if there is again closeness between you and the other person …

As a rule, with a moon love spell "eternal togetherness" is sought – but very rarely found. The greatest chance of success is given by such a spell, if it is performed in a general and manumitting way – but even then the "eternity" is by no means reliable.

II 4. Love

The love-dynamic of Venus is sometimes not easy to distinguish from the closeness-dynamic of the Moon. Most of the time there is a desire for closeness, but the feeling that the other person is "the only one" is more dominant – although sometimes this can hardly be distinguished from the desire for closeness.

When such a Venus love spell comes true, it often happens that the feelings and the interest wane again after a few weeks and one realizes that oneself and the other person are quite different and not as good a match as one had thought. This effect does not usually occur with a lunar theme – closeness continues to be sought even when the relationship is a disaster, because abandonment is the greatest fear of all for the person concerned (the "closeness-addict").

One can argue whether such a rather addictive longing for another person should be called "love" or not – the person in question himself will certainly name it this way …

II 5. Sex

The desire for sex has again a different dynamic, because it has a more ego-centered view – the other person is not seen so much as a human being, but rather as a "pleasure object". Therefore, the desire usually subsides quickly after a few nights together.

Another difference is that in the sex-love spells there are less addictive phenomena – according to the dynamics of Mars, there is more aggression, jealousy, greed, anger, ruthlessness, violence, and so on. Also a more frequent change of partners is to be expected.

Of course, this does not have to be the case, since Mars is first of all neutral in action – Mars is not brutal or ruthless out of itself, but only directed towards a goal that it wants to reach with all its might.

II 6. Communion

A love spell performed to obtain communion with a certain person is much rarer than the three motives mentioned before (closeness, love, sex).

In such a Jupiter love spell the same phenomenon will occur as in all love spells: When you summon another person, that person will mirror your own inner state to you – which is not always what you were looking for, but which is what can most effectively promote self-knowledge and self-healing …

II 7. Constancy

The search for permanence in a relationship, that is, the Saturn love spell, is hardly distinguishable from the Moon love spell. The Saturn love spell merely seeks permanence itself, the presence of a secure attachment figure, but not necessarily closeness as well, which is a lunar theme.

II 8. Polarities

The normal state of a person (or, if you will, the ideal state) is resting in oneself – inner fullness, then also clarity and strength, and at last radiance and self-love.

However, life is often a bit bumpy, so that sometimes one moves away from one's own center. This can happen in three areas: closeness (usually caused in the baby's oral phase), power (usually caused in the infant's anal phase), and self-love (usually caused in the child's phallic phase).

When something happens in one of these phases that the person has not been able to stomach effectively, he or she becomes either increasingly "loud" or increasingly "quiet" – and some people also constantly switch back and forth between these two extremes.

These three themes (closeness, power, self-love) and these three deviations (loud, quiet, switching) result in nine possible deviations from one's center. It is helpful to see whether one is resting in one's own center or whether one has possibly fallen out of one's own center and is now on one of these nine aberrations.

The Nine Aberrations				
Subject area		*Type of aberration*		
Topic	*possible problem*	*"loud"*	*"quiet"*	*switching between both*
closeness	lack	addict	ascetic	addict/ascetic
force	might	perpetrator	victim	perpetrator/victim
self-love	self-doubt	star	fan	star/fan

By the internal dynamics of these polarizations, addict and ascetic join together, as well as perpetrator and victim, and also star and fan – and then they perform together the drama of lack or violence or self-doubt. This is really no fun …

There are many forms in which these dramas can be performed: Addict and ascetic can choose the drama of "needy and helper", offender and victim can stage the tragedy of "violent and rape victim", and star and fan can perform, for example, the play of "delusions of grandeur and inferiority complexes". There are hardly any limits to creativity here – and the casual appearance of people who swing back and forth between two extremes only makes the whole thing more entertaining … but only if you are not part of such a drama yourself.

Magic only works when it is "charged" with enough power. So if an addict/perpetrator/star or an ascetic/victim/fan uses a love spell and there is enough power in that spell, that power will flow into the polarity between the addict/perpetrator/star and the ascetic/victim/fan, which will mainly lead to an increase in polarity to even greater extremes. One can actually only hope that the love spell will have no effect in this case, because otherwise the dilemma will only be intensified …

In such a polarization, in every person there is also the opposite pole to the extreme that this person lives outwardly: Every ascetic knows what addiction is, every addicts wants to be an ascetic at some times; every perpetrator fears to become a victim himself, every vitim has a lot of aggressions inside; every fan dreams of becoming a star himself, every star has hidden self-doubts. The polarization first takes place in one's own inner being, when the fullness in one's life is destoyed: The image of the addict and the ascetic, for example, arises in one's own inner being – which is why there are people who switch back and forth between the two extremes of a subject.

There is never switching back and forth between the extremes of two different subjects (e.g. between addict and perpetrator or between victim and star).

II 9.   The Relationship Mandala

The psyche has a simple fundamental stucture:

The identity of a person (soul) is his core.

Around this center is formed the image of the inner man and the inner woman – as a rule, with a man, the male image is the self-image and the female image is the search image. With the woman it is exactly the other way around.

Now, when polarization occurs, both images polarize – the inner man and the inner woman, resulting in a total of four polarized images.

Of these images, the person lives only one image – the other three images are taken over by other people like roles in a play.

This would look like the following overview for a man with a polarization of the closeness theme – the part that this man actually lives himself is highlighted in darker gray.

In this overview the ideal develepement of an addict is shown

The polarization dynamic and its healing						
Origin	*Unfolding*	*Polarization*	*Life*	*Realization*	*Healing*	*Being whole*
identity (soul)	inner man	he-addict	oneself	he-addict	inner man	identity (soul)
		he-ascetic	"enemy"	he-ascetic		
	inner woman	she-addict	"girlfriend"	she-addict	inner woman	
		she-ascetic	"relationship"	she-ascetic		

As a mandala, this structure can be represented as follows:

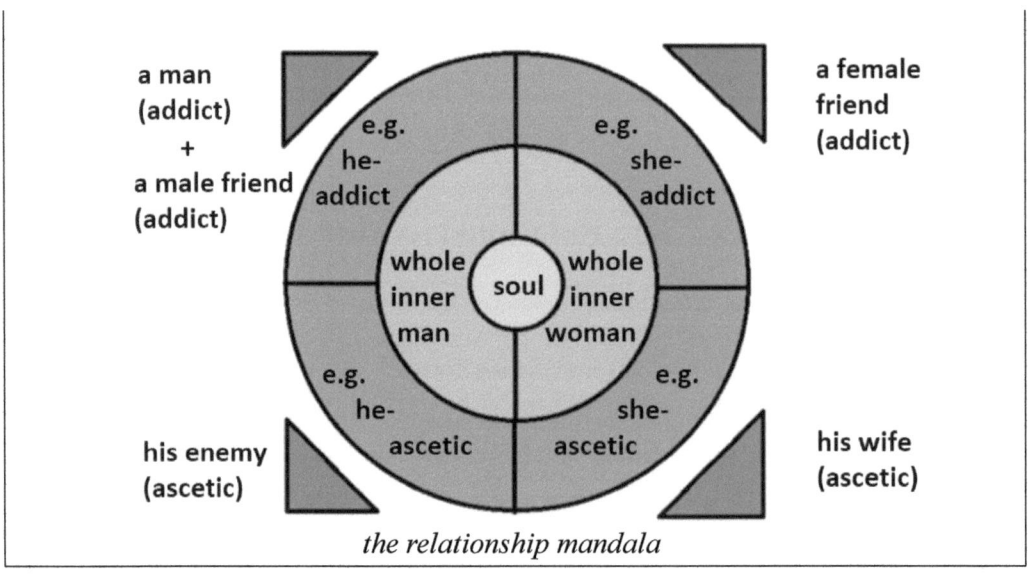

the relationship mandala

If one intends to perform a love spell, it may be useful to check whether one is reasonably close to one's own center – otherwise it could be that one only increases one's own addiction, struggle or self-doubt through the love spell and its consequences …

A full account of this mandala including its healing can be found in my book "Das Beziehungs-Mandala".

II 10. Chakras

One can also view a love spell from the chakra where someone has focused most of their attention:

- In the <u>heart chakra</u> lies identity – and consequently self-love.

- The <u>solar plexus</u> below the heart chakra is physical self-expression and the <u>throat chakra</u> above the heart chakra is social self-expression. In these two chakras, identity has become a general desire.
Therefore, these two chakras are the starting point for the general releasing love spells. From these chakras, an impulse is sent into the world that is a manumitting and general request, that is, an invitation.

- In the <u>hara</u> under the solar plexus lies inner support and in the <u>third eye</u> above the throat chakra lies outer orientation. In these two chakras, the general wish of the solar plexus and the throat chakra becomes a concrete wish that relates to a specific person.
Therefore, these two chakras are the starting point for the concrete love spells, in which the sorcerer takes a dominant position. From these two chakras emanates a power directed towards a specific person. This is the origin of the coercive love spells.

In the <u>root chakra</u> under the hara lies physical contact and in the <u>crown chakra</u> above the third eye lies spiritual contact. In these two chakras, the concrete desire of the hara and the third eye becomes an experience.
Therefore, these two chakras play a role especially in already existing relationships, in which the love spells shall determine future actions and future events.

- - -

One can also look at the chakras in another way, as they also reflect the polarization that was described in the previous chapter.

17

Root chakra and crown chakra

The closeness theme with its two extremes of the addict and the ascetic lies in the outer pair of chakras:

> The <u>addict</u> has a life force congestion in the root chakra and a life force deficiency in the crown chakra;
> the <u>ascetic</u> has a life-force congestion in the crown chakra and a life-force deficiency in the root chakra.

> > => The love spells made out of the feeling of a great lack refer to this pair of chakras – in the case of the addict as the search for concrete closeness, in the case of the ascetic as the adoration of a distant beloved.
> > The addiction/ascetic love spells start from these two chakras: the addiction from the root chakra, the asceticism from the crown chakra.
> > These love spells are about action in a single situation.

Hara and Third Eye

The power theme with its two extremes of the perpetrator and the victim lies in the middle pair of chakras:

> The <u>perpetrator</u> has a life force congestion in the hara and a life force deficiency in the third eye;
> the <u>victim</u> has a life-force congestion in the third eye and a life-force deficiency in the hara.

> > => The love spells that have to do with one's own wishes for a concrete person refer to this pair of chakras – in the case of the perpetrator as the assertion of one's own will and in the case of the victim as the desperate plea for kind attention.
> > The perpetrator/victim love spells emanate from these two chakras: the compulsion from the hara and the pleading from the third eye.
> > These love spells are about the relationship with a concrete person.

Solar plexus and throat chakra

The self-expression theme with its two extremes of the star and the fan lies in the inner pair of chakras:

> The star has a life force congestion in the solar plexus and a life force deficiency in the throat chakra;
> the fan has a life force congestion in the throat chakra and a life force deficiency in the solar plexus.

>> => The love spells that have to do with general desires relate to this pair of chakras – in the case of the star as the desire for admiration and in the case of the fan as a bashful looking up to the idol.
>> The star/fan love spells emanate from these two chakras: the admiration craving from the solar plexus and the subordination from the throat chakra.
>> These love spells are about the relationship with people in general.

Heart Chakra

Being anchored in the heart chakra is found in people who rest in their center.

From these connections it follows, among other things, that in the compulsion love spell the sorcerer gathers his life force in his hara (which he will most likely already do habitually) and from there compels the other person to do what he wants.

In the "craving for recognition"-love spell, on the other hand, the sorcerer will want to act from his solar plexus and put everyone under his spell.

The addiction-love spell, on the other hand, is performed by the sorcerer from his root chakra – a pull that draws everything to himself.

These are the three "loud" extremes.

The three "quiet" extremes are the ascetic, the victim and the fan.

In the adoring love dpell, the sorcerer is concentrated in his crown chakra.

In the supplication love spell, on the other hand, he is active almost only in his third eye.

Finally, the fan is entirely in his throat chakra during his shame love spell.

One can conclude from the type of love spell which chakra has to be used for it –

19

and one can also conclude from the chakra active in the love spell about the character of the love spell.

II 11. Oracle

An almost superfluous hint is the recommendation to consult one or another oracle such as the Tarot cards or the I Ching before performing a love spell. This does not mean at all that one should consult the oracle and not perform a love spell – but an action that is done out of a clarity about oneself and about the situation generally bears the most tasty fruits …

II 12. The own Horoscope

One's own horoscope can be a good help in assessing one's own situation correctly and in finding sensible behavior.

For relationships, the position of the three planets Moon (closeness), Venus (love) and Mars (sex) are especially important. For a lasting life relationship, on the other hand, Jupiter is of very great importance, which is responsible for values and life organization.

Since love spells are performed when one has a problem, one can also look at the squares, quincunxes and semisextiles in one's horoscope, since these aspects usually describe a person's problems.

These aspects have a widening, transforming and changing dynamic:

- The square separates two planets that want to develop and express themselves independently, but with consideration for each other. Here it is important not to get into an "either or". The square is like a tent pole that separates two things, but thereby creates a space.

- The quincunx is the constant change that comes from the fact that there are constantly new situations, new things are experienced and absorbed, other things are cleaned up, purified or discarded.… The present is constantly integrated into what already exists.

- The semisextile is the further development from one state to the next, following state – nothing remains as it is …

- Sometimes also the <u>opposition</u> is of importance: It is the constant change between two poles – in the ideal case a swinging seesaw.

These are only short hints – the detailed description of astrology would of course go beyond the scope of this book.

II 13. Dream journey

In order to understand a situation before one begins to act, one can also perform a dream journey on the subject in question or, on a dream journey, ask a deity to whose realm the subject in question belongs for advice and help.

II 14. Knowledge

Finally, one's own background knowledge and experience with the subject plays a major role: What does one know about relationships, about their dynamics, about horoscopes, about partner horoscopes, about the psychological dynamics of relationships, etc.? And what kind of relationships has one already experienced? How well does one know one's own biography and the imprint it has left on oneself? Has one resolved any existing traumas in one's own psyche?

Finally, there is a very important point: Everyone grows up in a certain family and culture and therefore has their parents and the standard relationship model from their own culture as a role model. However, there is a very wide variety of possible relationship models – both those from other cultures and from former times and also those that have been tried out in more recent times.

It is therefore highly recommended to have a look at some of these forms – simply to know the variety of possibilities and then to see which of these possibilities feels best. In this way, you gain a freedom of choice that you would not otherwise have …

It is not at all a matter of living the most exotic relationship model possible, but simply of acquiring the knowledge and courage to do what suits you best.

III Love Spells: Invitation

After examining your own situation and motivation more closely, you may come to the conclusion that you want to perform a love spell.

III 1. Planet dream journey

A relatively simple possibility for a love spell is the dream journey – if one already has some practice with this method. For example, one can travel to the planet that matches the character of one's desire, and then ask this planet for help.

Possibly you can also ask it for a comment on your intention – usually these comments are very unexpected, unpleasant … and helpful …

III 1. a) Moon

One would undertake a dream journey to the moon, if it is about closeness. It doesn't matter whether this is a dream journey consisting mainly of images or mainly of words – although images are more likely in this case.

In this case it is helpful to ask the moon also about one's own present relationship to closeness, to find out what one can do in one's own psyche or in one's own life to heal one's own relationship to closeness and thus to increase the chances of closeness also in the outside.

The probability that during such a dream journey also one's own mother and possibly also one's own father will play a role is quite high.

In this theme the root chakra and the crown chakra will probably be addressed.

III 1. b) Venus

A dream journey to Venus would be undertaken if it is about love. Again, it doesn't matter if this becomes a dream journey consisting primarily of images or primarily of words – the likelihood is about the same.

It is also helpful in this case to ask Venus also about one's present own relationship to love in general, in order to find out what one can do in one's own psyche or in one's own life to heal one's own relationship to love and thus to increase the chances also for the very concrete experience of love.

The probability of finding one's own inner search image during such a dream journey is quite high: thus, in the case of a man, the inner woman – and in the case of a woman, the inner man.

In this theme the solar plexus and the throat chakra are probably addressed above all, but possibly also the two outer chakras.

III 1. c) Mars

A dream journey to Mars would be undertaken if it is about sex. Again, there is no clear tendency for dream journeys to consist more of images or more of words, except for possibly very striking and drastic sayings of Mars.

In this case it is again helpful to ask Mars about one's own present relationship to sex, in order to find out what one can do in one's own or in one's own life to heal one's own relationship to sex and thus to increase the chances of having sex with another person.

The probability of finding one's own inner search image during such a dream journey is also quite high – however, it is even more important to find the self-image, since this self-image is active during sex: thus, in the case of a man, the inner man – and in the case of a woman, the inner woman.

In this theme, the root chakra and the crown chakra will probably be addressed most of all, and incidentally the hara and the third eye – the emphasis will probably be on the hara and the root chakra.

III 2. Planet rituals

While dream journeys are an inner encounter with the planets, rituals are an outer encounter with the planets. Since in a ritual one performs the actions oneself, while in a dream journey one is more aware than in a ritual, the ritual is more active and the dream journey more passive.

Consequently, the three "loud" extremes, i.e. the addict, the abuser and the star tend to rituals, while the three "quiet" extremes, i.e. the ascetic, the victim and the fan tend to dream journeys.

It would therefore be a good idea to use both in roughly equal measure and avoid one-sidedness.

III 2. a) Moon

One of the simplest forms of a lunar ritual consists of drawing a protective circle and then drawing the lunar hexagram (see sketch) in all four directions, top, bottom and center. This allows the room to be charged with the quality of the moon. Afterwards one pronounces one's wish to the moon.

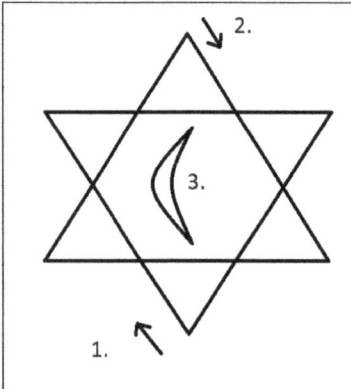	1. Draw the lower triangle in the air, starting in the direction of the arrow, imagining it; chant "Shaddai" while doing so. 2. Draw the upper triangle in the air starting in the direction of the arrow, imagining it and chanting "el-Chai". 3. Draw the moon symbol in the air while imagining it and chanting "Ararita".

This simple ritual can be completed by choosing a full moon night as date for the ritual, by burning suitable incense, by laying moonstones and opals and a silver chalice on the altar, by wearing ritual clothes, by using long moon-invocations and so on. This should be handled as it feels good.

It also depends mainly on one's own character and temperament whether one formulates the request to the moon beforehand and then recites it, or whether one prefers to improvise at that moment.

Of course, you can also perform this ritual in a clearing where the full moon is shining, possibly leaving out the lunar hexagrams.

If one wishes, one can also ask the Moon Archangel Gabriel for help. You can imagine Gabriel in a violett robe – he wears blue as the Archangel of Water and violet as the Archangel of the Moon, so to speak). It is useful to pay attention to whether he tells you something – just as you can hear him speak on a dream journey.

III 2. b) Venus

The Venus ritual can be performed in the same way, using the Venus hexagram.

One can also perform the ritual outside just after sunset or just before sunrise – depending on when Venus is currently visible in the sky.

If one wishes, one can also ask the Venus Archangel Haniel for help. You can imagine him in a green robe.

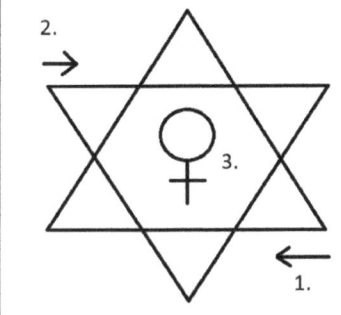	1. Draw the lower triangle in the air, starting in the direction of the arrow, while imagining it; chant "Yod-he-Vau-He". 2. Draw the upper triangle in the air starting in the direction of the arrow, imagining it and chanting "Tzabaoth". 3. Draw the Venus symbol in the air while imagining it, singing "Ararita".

III 2. c) Mars

One can also perform the Mars ritual in the same way, using the Mars hexagram.

One can also perform the ritual outside at night if Mars is visible in the sky.

If one wishes, one can also ask the Venus Archangel Samael for help. You can imagine him in a red robe.

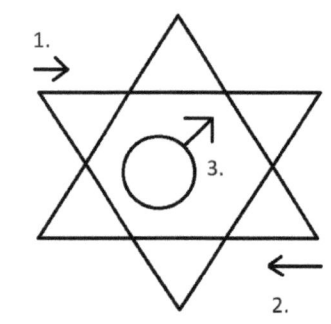

1. Draw the upper triangle in the air, starting in the direction of the arrow, imagining it, chanting "Elohim".

2. Draw the lower triangle in the air starting in the direction of the arrow, imagining it and chanting "Gibor".

3. Draw the Mars symbol in the air, imagining it and chanting "Ararita".

III 3.   Invocations

One can also make these rituals a bit more "personal" by invoking a deity either in addition to the hexagrams or instead of the hexagrams and the archangel.

For the moon, for example, Isis, Hathor, Inanna, Nanna, Pte-san-win and Kuan Yin would fit.

For Venus this would be mainly Freya and Aphrodite as well as the Dakinis, the Huris and the Valkyries.

To Mars correspond among others Pan, Priapos, Freyr and possibly also Shiva.

When choosing a deity, you should go by what feels good – and you should also stick to the style and culture that you are most familiar with or like most.

For Christian-oriented magicians there are books in which the "special fields" of the different saints are listed – there you can find for almost every need a responsible saint.

Sometimes, however, you have to look a little more closely to find out what the mostly somewhat outdated terms mean (e.g. "censoriousness" for exaggerated criticism or "television" for telepathy).

III 4.   One's own soul

In case of doubt, it is always useful to seek support from one's own soul, because one will hardly be able to carry out anything that contradicts what one's own soul wants. On the other hand, your own soul can also show you by which changes in the planned love spell, for example, the contradiction with other parts of your own psyche can be resolved. This can make a love spell much more effective.

Presumably, however, one will actually listen to one's own soul only if one either already rests quite well in one's own center or if one is completely desperate …

III 4. a)   Request to one's own soul

At this point you could take a dream journey to your own soul – or a dream journey to your own heart chakra or to your own center, which is ultimately all the same. Thereby one can possibly find out what one's own soul is actually up to in its current incarnation – which would certainly also make the dynamics of one's own relationships clearer.

One can also ask the soul directly for a fulfilling relationship – but it seems to be more skillful to ask it also for what it understands by this …

III 4. b)   Achieving inner freedom from contradictions

A point that one can well take care of oneself is the search for inner contradictions in relation to the topic of "relationships". It might be helpful to talk to a good friend about this and to look for such inner contradictions together – sometimes one is a little bit blind in emotionally charged topics …

If you find such contradictions (without the self-blockade by such contradictions you probably wouldn't even think about love spells), it is of course also useful to resolve them.

In many cases a change of perspective already helps, i.e. an attempt to see what the two halves of this contradiction actually want. For example, one half might strive for self-determination and the other for closeness – which one might experience as a contradiction. Both aspects can possibly be recognized as two sides of one's own self-expression – then one's own two fists no longer beat against each other, but one radiates from the heart again. Possibly the formulation "self-determination in a fulfilling relationship" could already help to soften the contradiction and take some of the pressure off the topic.

If there should be more violent contradictions, one usually gets further with the procedure "look, feel, embrace".

- The first of these steps means that you look as calmly and neutrally and objectively as possible at what exactly this contradiction looks like – in doing so, you will usually also be able to recognize how old you were when this feeling arose.

- The second step means that one sees that it is oneself who has this feeling that has led to this inner contradiction – and that one still carries this feeling within oneself. You should feel this old feeling only as long as you can "keep your head above water". Therefore, you may have to go to this feeling several times and feel it.

- The third step means that one sees this (suffering) "younger I", which has the age in which the feeling arose, standing opposite oneself – and one then embraces it.

Through these three steps, these old feelings are reintegrated – which significantly increases the chances that the love spells, which may be performed afterwards, will lead to pleasant results.

III 4. c)   Re-orientation

Probably the resolution of the inner contradiction will lead to changing one's perspective and finding a new question or a new request to one's soul.

It makes sense to examine this new question or request again for inner contradictions and possibly to apply the "look, feel, embrace" procedure once more.

III 4. d)   Silver cords

A general procedure to summon something you need are the silver cords – no matter if you are looking for a new tenant, want to meet new friends or find a parking space or even a relationship.

The process is very simple: imagine sending out life force strings from your own body, which find their way to what you want. Usually these silver cords emanate from one's own solar plexus.

These life-force cords, sometimes called "silver cords," actually look milky white and have a slight blue tinge – which, however, is very close to "silver."

III 4. e) One's own power animal

Possibly one's own power animal can also help, if one already knows it. It is also interesting to have a look at the behavior of one's own power animal with regard to living together (Moon) in the pack, in the herd, in the swarm etc. as well as the kind of bonds (Venus) that it forms and the form of sex (Mars) that is usual with it. Probably you will find many similarities to your own behavior.

Possibly also one's own power plant and the own power stone can tell you something about your relationships, although the power animal is usually the most important of these three allies in this topic, because the power animal clarifies the own dynamics. The power plant, on the other hand, is one's own attitude and the power stone is one's own structure.

III 4. f) Felix felicis

There is another very interesting and recommendable experiment with an imaginary potion. In the "Harry Potter" books, in the 6th volume, a magic potion called "Felix felicis" is described. Since these books have now exceeded the circulation of half a billion, the images from these books have also become quite thoroughly anchored in the collective subconscious.

If you know the golden-colored magic potion "Felix felicis" and its effect from the books, you can imagine once in the morning to take three drops of this potion. Then you speak out your wish – the on which gave you the idea to perform a love spell. See what the day will bring you …

(Also, on Ron Weasley, the potion only supposedly taken had the same effect as the potion actually taken).

It works.

IV Love Spells: Compulsion

The love spells in the previous chapter were general, manumitting spells that emanate from the solar plexus and the throat chakra.

In this chapter, the spells emanating from the Hara and the Third Eye are described.

IV 1. Risks of compulsion

The risk of compulsion spells is mainly that they might work. Because of the principle that a spell summons not only what one consciously invokes, but also everything that is associated with the subject in question, it could be that the result of the spell, while agreeing on the very literal level with the wish sent out, has one or two flaws that one does not like at all.

The most extreme case would be that, for example, a man who wants to have a certain woman and pulls her to him with all his might and then actually sees her again – but at her funeral in the morgue … Fortunately, only a few spells are so strong that they could create such an extreme result.

The second point about the compulsion spell is the compulsion itself, which is also found in the encounter that came about in this way:

- Does one want to be with someone whom one has forced to be with?
- Does one really want to make the other person an object of one's desire by the exercise of coercion?
- Does one want to be with the other person against the other person's will?
- Does one want to have a fight as the basis of a relationship?

One can have very different attitudes towards such a magical compulsion – but it is highly recommended to think about this kind of compulsion before performing a corresponding love spell.

A wide-known fictional example of the consequences of such a compulsive love-spell ist describe by J. K. Rowling: Lord Voldemort was born after his mother cast a compulsive love-spell on his father.

IV 2. Sigil magic

Sigil magic is a very simple, yet effective form of magic. In a love spell, the first thing you would do is to state what you want as succinctly as possible in a short sentence.

The following sentences are not suggestions for particularly well done sigil sentences, but rather drastically worded examples of how these sentences might sound at the six polar extremes.

- <u>Addict</u> (life force congestion in the root chakra): *"I want sex with him right now!"*

- <u>Ascetic</u> (life force congestion in the crown chakra): *"If only we could at least have a friendship!"*

- <u>Perpetrator</u> (life force congestion in the hara): *"Let her do what I want!"*

- <u>Victim</u> (life force congestion in the third eye): *"If he only could be a bid more kind to me."*

- <u>Star</u> (life force congestion in the solar plexus): *"Let the women all come to me!"*

- <u>Fan</u> (life force congestion in the throat chakra): *"If only a woman would speak to me for once!"*

This sentence (which should preferably not resemble any of the above sentences too closely) is written down, e.g.: "Ich will sex mit Peter." ("I want to have sex with Peter.")

Now cross out all the double letters from this sentence, "I wl sex mt Pr." So you are left with the following letters, "I wl sex mt pr."

From these letters, one now assembles a sigil and simplifies it until it has acquired a memorable shape. This process might look like the following:

The construction of the sigil				
i c h	*+ w + s + l*	*+ e + x*	*+ m + t*	*+ p + r*
1. simplification	*2. simplification*	*3. simplification*	*4. simplification*	*5. simplification*

Now follows the actual magical part, which consists in concentrating on this sigil either for a short time or for a while and then forgetting it.

Various methods can be used for this concentration: simple concentration and imagination, contemplation of the symbol in inner silence, auto-eroticism, pain, disgust, a loud cry – whatever feels good and whatever one wants to use.

IV 3.   Hypnosis and remote hypnosis

A very direct form of coercion is hypnosis. The classical form with lots of words is of course unsuitable here, as it would immediately attract attention. Remote hypnosis is more practical in this case, but it requires a little practice. In the end, fixed concentration on the goal is the most practical method.

One can combine single-mindedness on one's goal with unobtrusively speaking some words describing one's goal – the words are in sentences that are about something completely different. In these words you put your will and direct the other person's subconscious mind to where you want him to go.

This can be completely unobtrusive and yet very effective. Of course, it is difficult when you not only have to bend the circumstances a little, but when the other person wants something completely different than you do.

In principle, in hypnosis, in remote hypnosis and in "hypnotic conversation", the most effective attitude is the calm conviction that exactly what one wants will happen. This attitude can also be experienced in meditation – it is an inner vibration that stabilizes itself.

Of course, this only works if you have no inner contradiction to what you are doing. If one has e.g. moral doubts against one's own action, one might as well leave this kind of magic alone …

IV 4.   Woodoo dolls

A quite well known method is the Woodoo doll. This is a doll that represents the one you want to attract to yourself. In order for the spell to work with this doll, it should contain a hair, a piece of cut off fingernail or something similar from the person in question.

Now you can make a play with this doll, so to speak, and represent how it comes running to you and how you do with it what you want to do. In the more brutal methods, a rope is placed around the neck of this doll, by which the doll (and consequently the person in question) is then pulled towards the magician.

IV 5. Menstrual blood and sperm

A completely different approach, known from many cultures, is to make a magical connection without a Woodoo doll. In this case the connection is made in the other direction than with the Woodoo doll: the magician or witch sends a part of himself or herself to the person who is to be drawn near.

The most popular method is for the witch to mix some of her menstrual blood into the food of the man in question, or for the magician to mix some of his sperm into the food of the woman in question. On the basis of this connection it is then imagined that one pulls the person concerned to oneself. Another possibility would be to use this connection to send the image of erotic desire for oneself to the person in question.

This method is tricky if the man or woman who is to be forced in this way to behave in a certain way knows something about magic himself. In this case, the "victim" could use this connection to harm the "perpetrater". In doing so, the "victim" would be in the stronger position, since she carries a part of the sorcerer within herself and is therefore superior to the sorcerer – she can now "eat" the sorcerer.

IV 6. Spiritus familiaris

A somewhat more cumbersome but effective method is to make a spirit to perform the love spell.

For such a spirit, one mixes two parts of yellow clay with one part of beeswax, melts this mixture in a pot and forms from it the shape that the spirit is to receive – e.g. a cat. In this cat is pressed a hole at least 5cm deep.

Now boil a chamomile flower decoction (very strong tea) and add a few drops of Aurum chloratum C200 (a homeopathic remedy). This liquid is poured into the hole in the cat, a few drops of one's own blood are added and then the hole is sealed with a clay/wax plug.

Now the cat gets a name and is charged daily with the elements fire, water, air, earth and light by holding your hand over the cat and imagining life force flowing into this cat in the form of the four elements plus the quintessence (light).

After a few weeks, one can then send this cat, i.e. the spirit of this cat, off to perform tasks – such as summoning a certain person.

Such a spirit, however, after a short time, becomes like a pet that you don't want to miss – after all, it consists of your own seperated life force. Since such a spirit can become more and more independent in the course of time, one must dissolve it again at some point – which can feel like the murder of a beloved pet.

So this method has advantages and disadvantages …

IV 7. Planetary rituals in another attitude

The planetary rituals already described can also be performed with a different basic attitude, not inviting something freely, but charging oneself with the power of the selected planet and then with this power commanding a certain event to happen.

This method must suit you, otherwise you cannot perform it. If one looks up to the planets reverently as to gods, this procedure will hardly be feasible. If one looks at the planets more technically, the "planetary compulsion" method fits better.

IV 8. Io Pan!

The request to Pan for help is something in between a manumitting invitation and a coercion.

Pan's method is quite simple: He chooses a suitable woman and then sends her e.g. intense erotic dreams of the magician who asked Pan for help. Then this woman is filled with disere for this man.

The same, of course, can be done by a witch in relation to a man.

V   Protection against love spells

After having described in the previous chapter what magicians can do to make another person do what the magician wants, the countermeasures follow in this chapter.

One could argue, of course, that it would be better if no one knew these methods, but since anyone can find them out who cares to, it is better to know these methods. However, this knowledge is not so widespread as to be common knowledge – it is more common to specialists in the field.

It would certainly not make sense to think of black magic every time you find something strange and odd – this way you can become very quickly and thoroughly mentally ill. One should always rule out all other, "natural" explanations before thinking about whether something could have been caused by magic.

Magic works, that's no question – but persecution mania can also become out-spoken real …

So stay calm and in your own center.

It is also not wrong to do a dream journey in case of a well-founded suspicion of a magical attack, in order to possibly find out something more detailed – but also here one should be careful with the interpretation of what one has seen on the dream journey and not draw any hasty conclusions, because it is much easier to get wrong ideas than to get rid of them again.

V 1.   Radiance in self-fidelity

The surest protection is "radiating in self-trust" – then there is no "gateway" for external attacks and then no one will even think of performing a love spell against the "radiating person" in question.

Every external attack needs a lack, a fear or a self-doubt in the attacked person to be able to start the attack at this weak point. To attack someone who has no such weak point is extremely troublesome.

Probably the "radiant people" will not even think of taking a book like this about the love spells in their hands and reading it – they simply don't need it …

V 2. Pyramid

A simple form of a protection spell is the imagination of a golden shining pyramid, in the middle of which you stand. This image is simple and you can imagine it quickly. This protective and purifying image originates from the late Cypriot healer Daskalos – at least I got to know it through him.

This light pyramid is not a differentiated protection spell, nor is it a cleansing that covers all details, but it is extremely effective and useful as a first aid.

V 3. Middle Pillar

The "Middle Pillar Exercise" is widely used and extremely effective and applicable in wide range of situations. It is, so to speak, a "quick invocation of God". One imagines the glistening white light as which one can perceive God in visions; then one imagines this light flowing down from above and filling oneself with this light.

The Middle Pillar is a part of the Kabbalistic Tree of Life. The five names of God that one chants aloud or even inwardly in this method correspond to the five areas on this pillar. These areas are imagined as five balls of light with different colors.

One begins with the imaginations and the chanting at the top and ends at the bottom. These imaginations and names of God from the Old Testament are:

The Middle Pillar				
Area	*Meaning*	*Color*	*Place*	*Name of God*
Kether	God	white	above the head	Eheieh
Da'ath	protective deity	rainbow	neck	Yod-He-Vau-He Elohim
Tiphareth	soul	golden	heart chakra	Yod-He-Vau-He Eloa va-Da'ath
Yesod	life force	violet	genitals	Schaddai el-Chai
Malkuth	body	brown	under the feet	Adonai ha-Aretz

This „meditative ritual" or „ritual meditation" is done quite easily:

First, one imagines the glistening white ball of light of Kether above one's head and chants (intones, vibrates) the name of God *"Eheieh"*.

Next, one imagines that the light of the white ball of Kether above one's head flows down to Da'ath in the throat area, thereby purifying Da'ath and unfolding there again its original quality as rainbow light. In the process, one chants *"Yod-He-Vau-He Elohim."*

Then the light flows from Da'ath to Tiphareth in the chest, purifying that area and allowing its original quality to shine there again in golden light. At the same time, one chants *"Yod-He-Vau-He Eloa va-Da'ath."*

Then the light flows on to Yesod in the hip area, where it shines violet. At the same time, one chants *"Shaddai el-Chai."*

Finally, it flows down to Malkuth under the feet, and there it again causes the same thing: the purification of the area and the unfolding of the original quality in this area – this one in brown light. At the same time one sings *"Adonai ha-Aretz"*.

The "Exercise of the Middle Pillar" is at the same time a purification, a protection, a charging with power and an invocation – thus a blessing in a comprehensive sense.

The use of the "Middle Pillar Exercise" is extremely beneficial in almost all magical operations.

V 4. Purification

It is also possible to perform a specific purification of one's own life-force body, but this is a complex matter and cannot be described comprehensive in a nutshell. The essential tools for this are

- feeling into the life force body of the one who is to be cleansed,
- the removal of all foreign "life force substances", and
- charging with life force e.g. by the Middle Pillar.

A rather unspecific form of purification and also of prevention is the "Lesser Pentagram Ritual" – especially if it is performed daily. This ritual creates a clear "life force boundary", through which nothing can easily penetrate from the outside to the inside.

A very specific form of cleansing is to see if you can perceive a connection from your own life force body to the outside, which leads to another person with whom you do not want to be connected – and who may have performed a love spell against you.

However, one should be very careful with the diagnosis "problems caused by a magical attack" – it is very easy to get into something, which is not good for the state of the psyche at all …

If someone has indeed magically established a connection to you in order to cast a love spell through this connection, you can see this connection internally as a life force cord, which usually leads from your own solar plexus to the solar plexus of the other person.

Not every such "umbilical cord" or "silver cord" is something harmful – for example, a mother also has such a connection to her child. By this telepathic bond a mother can feel e.g. when her child is in danger.

The connection in itself is not bad – but it can be used for beneficial or harmful purposes.

If you want to dissolve such a connection, you can proceed as follows:

- One examines to whom this silver cord leads.

- You check what happens in this silver cord and from where to where in it possibly life force is flowing.

- One decides whether one wants to have this connection or not.

- If you don't want to have it anymore, you take the silver cord in your hand a hand's width in front of your body (gestures with your hand and imagination) and cut it with a (real) knife or sword.

- One brings the end of this silver cord to Mother Earth and gives it to her to take care of this cord, of the person at its other end and of his situation. If one would not bring this cut silver cord to her, the end would get stuck again to oneself or to another person.

- One rubs dragon's blood (resin from the dragon tree) on the place where one has cut this silver cord (usually the solar plexus).

- Draw a protective sign (pentagram, cross, etc.) on the skin with your finger.

V 5.   Power animal

When dealing with life force issues, it is always helpful to call your power animal and see what it says, does or advises you. There is a good chance that you will learn something in this way that you have not yet seen or thought of.

Possibly you can also ask your power plant and your power stone for advice and help.

V 6.   The "light explosion"

There is a simple but effective method of self-protection: the light explosion. For this, one calls up God's light in oneself or imagines a glistening white light in oneself. One connects this light with one's own soul in one's heart chakra – and then lets this light explode, i.e. radiate outwards with a tremendous force.

This "light explosion" can be experienced on the Tree of Life in the Sephirah Chokmah as a "light storm": completely unhindered self-expression and self-expansion. (For the physicists and astronomers: This corresponds to the expansion of the universe with 10^{50}-times the speed of light right after the Big Bang, which is called "inflation of the universe".)

This method is the most violent thing one can do for self-protection – it is not differentiated to the external circumstances, but it is a boundless, liberating "I!!!"

It can inwardly have the force of an atomic bomb …

VI The Sun Love Spell

If one should have a problem with relationships (which would be conceivable with a reader of this book …), there is the possibility to start at different places:

- Heart Chakra: This possibility has not been discussed yet and is the subject of this chapter. Here the love spell starts from one's own identity.

- Solar Plexus and Throat Chakra: From these two chakras, relationships can be invited into one's life. This is the general, manumitting form of love spells.

- Hara and Third Eye: From these two chakras, someone concrete can be made to perform certain actions. This is the concrete, compelling form of love spells, which is directed at already existing connections, that is, which wants to shape the relationship with a concrete person – in a one-sided way.

- Root Chakra and Crown Chakra: From these two chakras the concrete action within a relationship starts. So the subject of these two chakras is not the love spell to create a relationship, and also not the question how to create a relationship with a concrete person, but just the problems in an existing relationship … which are not the primary subject of this little book.

To summarize once again:

- Heart chakra: one's own identity – self-love

- Solar Plexus and Throat Chakra: inviting a relationship into one's life

- Hara and Third Eye: the establishment of a relationship with a concrete person

- Root Chakra and Crown Chakra: actions in an already existing relationship.

VI 1.   Contemplation

In general (and before you start with a love spell) you can think about or feel into yourself and find out what the ideal relationship would look like for you.

In a second step you can think about your own style in general (e.g. with the help of your own horoscope). This style should then be included in the formulation of one's own ideal relationship.

In a third step you can see if you have considered all aspects:

- Moon: closeness, emotional security
- Mercury: conversations, understanding
- Venus: love, harmony, beauty
- Sun: self-confidence, self-expression, appreciation of individuality
- Mars: sex, action, tension, excitement
- Jupiter: goals, organization of life, enjoyment
- Saturn: constancy, reliability
- Uranus: novelty, surprises, spontaneity
- Neptune: magic, mysticism, art, ecology, fantasy
- Pluto: essentials, transformations, intensity

In a fourth step, one can then look at what previous relationships have looked like. This can reveal where the "knots" are that still need to be untied.

In a fifth step, one can then once again clarify which possibilities there actually are in order to check on the basis of this whether one has really already found one's ideal image of a relationship. A few such possibilities are:

- a man and a woman
- a couple, but also other encounters
- patchwork family
- no regular ties at all
- two couples together
- a couple, but always only for a certain period of time
- a community with the women as the center, who have loose relationships with all the men
- one man and one woman-harem
- one woman and one man-harem

- children with the mother
- children with mother and father
- children with the father
- children with the community
  etc.

There are a lot more possibilities. This enumeration of possibilities may help to see clearer, what the ideal state in relationships would be. If you do not see the possibilities and if you do not become creative, you do not see your freedom of choice.

Yo may simple choose "one man and one woman lifelong" – but it is a different thing if you choose this after pondering all the possibilities or if you choose this just because your parents did the same.

VI 2. The relationship mandala

In an earlier chapter of this book, the relationship mandala has already been presented. This mandala looks as follows:

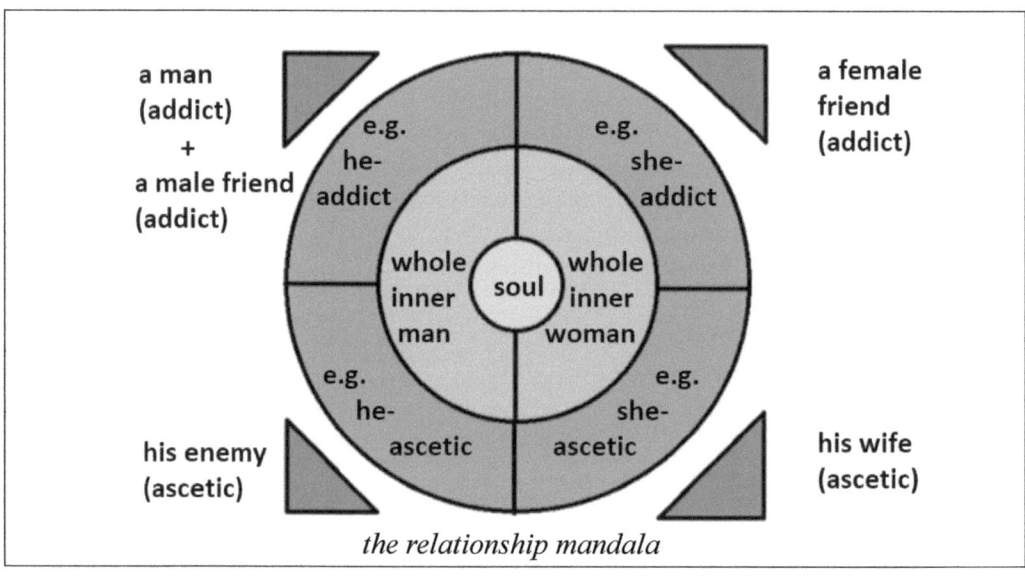

the relationship mandala

The center in this mandala is she soul in the heart chakra, which can also be called the "sun chakra" because of its central position. The soul is one's own identity.

The inner man and the inner woman are the two mirror images of the soul in the life force – they are the original, whole images of man and woman that one wants to live and experience in one's current life. Therefore, any love spell is ultimately about these two images.

The essential quality of the soul is boundless self-love. Since both the inner man and the inner woman are mirror images of the soul, the inner man and the inner woman love each other: This love is the reflection of the soul's self-love – it is the soul's self-love that also envelops its two mirror images.

The love between the inner man and the inner woman is the source of love for other people – ultimately, love for another person is an expression of the soul's self-love. Through love for another person, the soul can experience its own self-love on the outside …

The easiest way to get to know the inner man and the inner woman is to draw the central circle and the inner circle ring of the relationship mandala on the floor (e.g. with a woolen thread) or to mark them in another way (e.g. three pieces of paper with writing on it) and then to stand on these three positions one after the other like in a family constellation.

Another possibility would be two dream journeys to the inner man and to the inner woman.

VI 3.   The invocation of the inner couple

One can invoke this inner couple into oneself with an invocation. The inner man and the inner woman are of course already in you, but they may not be as conscious as they could be – and as it would be beneficial for your own relationships.

There is not much that can be said about this invocation … If you got to know them by a constellation, a dream journey or similar, you can simply call them up in yourself, address them and ask them to suffuse you, to tell you something or to show you something or to guide you through the day etc.. There are no limits to your own creativity here.

You can do this with the inner man as well as with the inner woman. Most of the time one tends to favor one of the two, but it is the presence of both that leads to real healing and abundance. When both the inner man and the inner woman are consciously present in oneself, relationships cease to be a "need" and become something to enjoy and something by which one can express oneself.

VI 4.   The inner couple meditation

The following meditation is the core of Tantra Yoga, which appears in various forms in the different traditions.

- One sits in a comfortable posture.

- One imagines the seven main chakras as lotus flowers: the root chakra, the hara, the solar plexus, the heart chakra, the throat chakra, the third eye and the crown chakra.

Inhaling, one speaks inwardly once "soul" (or its name if one knows it) or the name of a deity one relies on or simply "life". When breathing out, one speaks "life" or "love" each time.

One can also use a different mantra instead of the second word for each chakra, describing the healing state of that chakra. Then these mantras could be e.g. as follows

- crown chakra:	"Life" – "Unity"
- third eye:	"Life" – "Clarity"
- throat chakra:	"Life" – "Community"
- heart chakra:	"Life" – "Identity"
- solar plexus:	"Life" – "Radiance"
- hara:	"Life" – "Power"
- root chakra:	"Life" – "Ecstasy"

- One imagines the inner man and the inner woman sitting on the lotus flower in front of each other, one after the other, in the seven chakras.

- The inner man and the inner woman join hands and move towards each other. The inner woman sits on the man's lap and wraps her legs around his hips and both unite.

One feels into the inner woman and the inner man who have appeared (sevenfold) in the seven chakras and feels their union and their "feeling and loving each other."

- One remains in this state as long as one wishes. It may take several attempts before one can "bear" this state for a longer time, as there can be an unusual fullness and intensity in it.

- - -

If this meditation is too complex for you, you can first use a simplified version and only imagine the inner man and the inner woman in yourself and not consider the chakras. In this version, the inner man and woman unite only once and not seven times in the seven main chakras.

VI 5. Tantra

This ritual (sexual union) can also be performed as a couple, although it is advisable to avoid orgasm and instead keep the tension. It is not necessary to sit in the lotus position – it is enough to lie still together and move only enough to keep the tension. Most of the time, however, should consist only of lying still and feeling.

This "couple yoga" can also lead to the awakening of the Kundalini, which, however, is not the central concern in connection with love spells – although the awakening of the Kundalini would ultimately, of course, free one oneself and also the inner man and woman from all addictions, fears and misconceptions.

About this simple ritual there a lot of books …

VI 6. The sun love spell

The actual, really effective love spell is very simple:

- One goes inwardly to one's heart chakra and connects there with one's soul.

- One contemplates how the soul is reflected in the life force as one's inner man and woman.

- Then one lets these two, i.e. the inner man and the inner woman, shine outwards into the world like the sun.

This creates
fullness	instead of neediness and asceticism,
strength	instead of power and powerlessness,
self-love	instead of delusions of grandeur or inferiority complexes

and one attracts people who also live in abundance, strength and self-love … and can then have creative relationships with them.

- - -

If one wishes, one can also create and strengthen this radiance by a ritual:

    - One stands in the center of the relationship mandala that one has marked on the floor and connects with one's own soul.

    - One goes into the half-circle ring of the inner man and connects with him.

    - One goes into the half-circle ring of the inner woman and connects with her.

    - Then one takes the quality of these three and carries it to the east with a fitting gesture and lets it radiate out into the world.
This gesture is repeated to the south, west and north.

The attitude in this ritual is "radiant, unhindered self-expression." One radiates what one is into the world, and welcomes what comes towards one in response.

This is not a summoning, which is supposed to eliminate a lack, but a welcoming of what comes out of oneself – what comes as an echo, as a mirror-image out of the world, when one radiates into the world. In this gesture there is also no pressure and no pull, but a dance of one's own strength. This gesture is also not a request for recognition or an admiration of others, but a celebration of one's own self-love.

This gesture is simply radiating who you are. In this way, enriching and fulfilling relationships can emerge.

English Books by Harry Eilenstein

- Living Magic (261 p.)
- The Synthesis of Physics and Magic (192 p.)
- Telepathy for Beginners (60 p.)
- Telepathy for Advanced Learners (52 p.)
- Telekinesis for Beginners (56 p.)
- Astral Projection for Beginners (60 p.)
- Prophecy for Beginners (60 p.)
- Invocations for Beginners (52 p.)
- Evocations for Beginners (62 p.)
- Auto-Movement for Beginners (60 p.)
- Elves for Beginners (56 p.)
- Hypnosis for Beginners (56 p.)
- Love Magic for Beginners (52 p.)
- Money Magic for Beginners (60 p.)
- Magic Objects for Beginners (64 p.)
- Shamanism for Beginners (52 p.)
- Self Knowledge for Beginners (60 p.)
- Number Symbolism for Beginners (64 p.)
- Mandalas for Beginners (76 p.)

- Crop Circles for Beginners (344 p.)

These books will be puplished soon:

- Life Force for Beginners
- Meditation for Beginners
- Kundalini for Beginners
- Chakra-Magic for Beginners
- Astrology for Beginners
- Ritual Magic for Beginners
- Magic Research for Beginners
- Symbolism of Numbers for Beginners
- Language of the Moon – for Beginners
- Magic Chant for Beginners
- Da'ath-Magic for Beginners
- Feng Shui for Beginners
- Magic for Beginners – Anthology I
- Magic for Beginners – Anthology II
- Magic for Beginners – Anthology III
- Magic for Beginners – Anthology IV

Bücher von Harry Eilenstein

Religion allgemein
- Die sieben Schritte des Lebens (428 S.)
- Muttergöttin und Schamanen (168 S.)
- Göbekli Tepe (472 S.)
- Die Göttin von Göbekli Tepe (144 S.)
- Totempfähle (440 S.)
- Christus (60 S.)
- Dakini (80 S.)
- Vajra (76 S.)

Ägypten
- Hathor und Re 1: Götter und Mythen im Alten Ägypten (432 S.)
- Hathor und Re 2: Die altägyptische Religion – Ursprünge, Kult und Magie (396 S.)
- Isis (508 S.)

Indogermanen
- Die Entwicklung der indogermanischen Religionen (700 S.)
- Wurzeln und Zweige der indogermanischen Religion (224 S.)

Germanen
- Die Götter der Germanen (87 Bände – siehe nächste Seite)
- Odin (300 S.)

Kelten
- Cernunnos (690 S.)
- Taliesin (228 S.)
- Der Kessel von Gundestrup (220 S.)
- Der Chiemsee-Kessel (76)

Psychologie
- Über die Freude (100 S.)
- Das Geheimnis des inneren Friedens (252 S.)
- Das Beziehungsmandala (52 S.)
- Gefühle und ihre Verwandlungen (404 S.)
- einsgerichtet (140 S.)
- Liebe und Eigenständigkeit (216 S.)
- Von innerer Fülle zu äußerem Gedeihen (52 S.)

Heilung
- Die Symbolik der Krankheiten (76 S.)

Kunst
- Herz des Tanzes – Tanz des Herzens (160 S.)

Drama
- König Athelstan (104 S.)

Bücher von Harry Eilenstein

„Magie für Anfänger"

- Telepathie für Anfänger (60 S.)
- Telepathie für Fortgeschrittene (52 S.)
- Telekinese für Anfänger (52 S.)
- Lebenskraft für Anfänger (60 S.)
- Meditation für Anfänger (56 S.)
- Kundalini für Anfänger (100 S.)
- Hypnose für Anfänger (56 S.)
- Auto-Movement für Anfänger (56 S.)
- Chakra-Magie für Anfänger (148 S.)
- Astralreisen für Anfänger (56 S.)
- Astrologie für Anfänger (120 S.)
- Ritual-Magie für Anfänger (56 S.)
- Mandalas für Anfänger (68 S.)
- Geldzauber für Anfänger (56 S.)
- Liebeszauber für Anfänger (52 S.)
- Invokationen für Anfänger (52 S.)
- Evokationen für Anfänger (60 S.)
- Elfen für Anfänger (56 S.)
- Magie-Forschung für Anfänger (140 S.)
- Selbsterkenntnis für Anfänger (52 S.)
- Zahlensymbolik für Anfänger (60 S.)
- Die Sprache des Mondes – für Anfänger (116 S.)
- Zaubergesänge für Anfänger (100 S.)
- Zukunftschau für Anfänger (60 S.)
- Schamanismus für Anfänger (52 S.)
- Magische Gegenstände für Anfänger (68 S.)
- Da'ath-Magie für Anfänger (64 S.)
- Kornkreise für Anfänger (348 S.)
- Feng Shui für Anfänger (96 S.)
- Magie für Anfänger – Sammelband I (696 S.)
- Magie für Anfänger – Sammelband II (664 S.)
- Magie für Anfänger – Sammelband III (580 S.)

„Traumreisen"

- Traumreisen zu Heilpflanzen (700 S.)

Magie

- Handbuch für Zauberlehrlinge (408 S.)
- Tarot (104 S.)
- Physik und Magie (184 S.)
- Die Synthese von Physik und Magie (200S.)
- Die Magie-Formel (156 S.)
- Krafttiere – Tiergöttinnen – Tiertänze (112 S.)
- Schwitzhütten (524 S.)
- Mythen und Magie der Harfe (116 S.)
- Magie heute – Berichte aus der Praxis (288 S.)

Meditation

- Der Lebenskraftkörper (230 S.)
- Die Chakren (100 S.)
- Das Chakren-System mit den Nebenchakren (296 S.)
- Organe und Chakren (64 S.)
- Die platonischen Körper in den Chakren (156 S.)
- Meditation (140 S.)
- Drachenfeuer (124 S.)
- Kundalini I (676 S.)
- Reinkarnation (156 S.)
- einsgerichtet (140 S.)

Astrologie

- Astrologie (496 S.)
- Photo-Astrologie (428 S.)
- Die astrologischen Aspekte (88 S.)
- Horoskop und Seele (120 S.)

Kabbala

- Kursus der praktischen Kabbala (150 S.)
- Eltern der Erde (450 S.)
- Blüten des Lebensbaumes:
    - Die Struktur des kabbalistischen Lebensbaumes (370 S.)
    - Der kabbalistische Lebensbaum als Forschungshilfsmittel (580 S.)
    - Der kabbalistische Lebensbaum als spirituelle Landkarte (520 S.)

Die Themen der 87 Bände der Reihe „Die Götter der Germanen"

1. Die Entwicklung der germanischen Religion
2. Lexikon der germanischen Religion
3. Der ursprüngliche Göttervater Tyr
4. Tyr in der Unterwelt: der Schmied Wieland
5. Tyr in der Unterwelt: der Riesenkönig Teil 1
6. Tyr in der Unterwelt: der Riesenkönig Teil 2
7. Tyr in der Unterwelt: der Zwergenkönig
8. Der Himmelswächter Heimdall
9. Der Sommergott Baldur
10. Der Meeresgott: Ägir, Hler und Njörd
11. Der Eibengott Ullr
12. Die Zwillingsgötter Alcis
13. Der neue Göttervater Odin Teil 1
14. Der neue Göttervater Odin Teil 2
15. Der Fruchtbarkeitsgott Freyr
16. Der Chaos-Gott Loki
17. Der Donnergott Thor
18. Der Priestergott Hönir
19. Die Göttersöhne
20. Die unbekannteren Götter
21. Die Göttermutter Frigg
22. Die Liebesgöttin: Freya und Menglöd
23. Die Erdgöttinnen
24. Die Korngöttin Sif
25. Die Apfel-Göttin Idun
26. Die Hügelgrab-Jenseitsgöttin Hel
27. Die Meeres-Jenseitsgöttin Ran
28. Die unbekannteren Jenseitsgöttinnen
29. Die unbekannteren Göttinnen
30. Die Nornen
31. Die Walküren
32. Die Zwerge
33. Der Urriese Ymir
34. Die Riesen
35. Die Riesinnen
36. Mythologische Wesen
37. Mythologische Priester und Priesterinnen
38. Sigurd/Siegfried
39. Helden und Göttersöhne
40. Die Symbolik der Vögel und Insekten
41. Die Symbolik der Schlangen, Drachen und Ungeheuer
42.a Die Symbolik der Herdentiere I
42.b Die Symbolik der Herdentiere II
43. Die Symbolik der Raubtiere
44. Die Symbolik der Wassertiere und sonstigen Tiere
45. Die Symbolik der Pflanzen
46. Die Symbolik der Farben
47. Die Symbolik der Zahlen
48. Die Symbolik von Sonne, Mond und Sternen
49.a Das Jenseits I – Das Hügelgrab
49.b Das Jenseits II – Der Jenseitsweg
50. Seelenvogel, Utiseta und Einweihung
51. Wiederzeugung und Wiedergeburt
52. Elemente der Kosmologie
53. Der Weltenbaum
54. Die Symbolik der Himmelsrichtungen und der Jahreszeiten
55.a Mythologische Motive I
55.b Mythologische Motive II
56. Der Tempel
57. Die Einrichtung des Tempels
58. Priesterin – Seherin – Zauberin – Hexe
59. Priester – Seher – Zauberer
60. Rituelle Kleidung und Schmuck
61. Skalden und Skaldinnen
62 Kriegerinnen und Ekstase-Krieger
63. Die Symbolik der Körperteile
64.a Magie und Ritual I
64.b Magie und Ritual II
64.c Magie und Ritual III
65. Gestaltwandlungen
66.a Magische Angriffs-Waffen
66.b Magische Verteidigungs-Waffen
67. Magische Werkzeuge und Gegenstände
68. Zaubersprüche
69. Göttermet
70. Zaubertränke
71. Träume, Omen und Orakel
72. Runen
73. Sozial-religiöse Rituale
74. Weisheiten und Sprichworte
75. Kenningar
76. Rätsel
77. Die vollständige Edda des Snorri Sturluson
78. Frühe Skaldenlieder
79.a Mythologische Sagas I
79.b Mythologische Sagas II
80. Hymnen an die germanischen Götter